HOW THEY LIVED

A CHILD IN VICTORIAN LONDON

EDWINA CONNER

Illustrated by
Mark Bergin

HOW THEY LIVED

An American Pioneer Family
A Child in Victorian London
A Colonial American Merchant
A Crusading Knight
An Edwardian Household
A Family in the Fifties
A Family in World War II
An Ice Age Hunter
An Inca Farmer
An Indian Brave

A Medieval Serf
A Plantation Slave
A Roman Centurion
A Samurai Warrior
A Saxon Farmer
A Slave in Ancient Greece
A Tudor Merchant
A Victorian Factory Worker
A Viking Sailor

First published in 1986 by
Wayland (Publishers) Limited
61 Western Road, Hove
East Sussex BN3 1JD, England

British Library Cataloguing in Publication Data
Conner, Edwina
A child in Victorian London. — (How they lived)
1. Great Britain — Social conditions — 19th century
I. Title   II. Series
942.081   HN385

ISBN 0 85078 644 4

Typeset by Planagraphic Typesetters Limited
Printed and bound in Belgium
by Casterman S.A.

CONTENTS

TWO NATIONS 4

LONDON — 'THE BIG SMOKE' 6

AT HOME 8

GOING TO SCHOOL 10

HEALTH AND DISEASE 12

AT WORK 14

FOOD AND COOKING 16

CLOTHES 18

THE LAW 20

BARNARDO'S HOMES 22

HAVING FUN 24

THE GREAT EXHIBITION 26

A DAY AT THE SEASIDE 28

THE END OF AN ERA 30

GLOSSARY 31

MORE BOOKS TO READ 31

INDEX 32

TWO NATIONS

Billy was exhausted, covered in soot and aching from head to toe. His elbows and knees were rubbed raw. There was blood running down his leg. He had a terrible cough and found it difficult to breathe. Sweeping chimneys was a dirty and dangerous job. Now he was on his way home in the dark.

His path took him down a smart street, and he couldn't resist looking in the window of a large house. It was warm and welcoming inside. He saw two children who were beautifully dressed: the boy in a velvet suit with a white collar and the girl in a pretty, long blue dress. They were sitting at a table with a man and a woman and there was such a feast laid out before them: sandwiches, meat and cakes! Billy's mouth watered and he sighed. Waiting for him, if he was lucky, would be a bowl of thin soup and a slice of dry bread.

Benjamin Disraeli (1804-81), Prime Minister during part of Queen Victoria's reign (1837-1901), once said that Britain was like two nations, or countries, not one: the 'privileged' or the rich, and the 'people', the poor. He meant that there was a very great difference between the two.

There was no welfare state in those days. The government did not provide council houses, no one was entitled to free health care and until 1870

there were very few schools. Poor families lived in very squalid conditions. Yet Britain was becoming an important industrial country, building more and more factories, ships and railways. Many people were making their fortunes.

During Victorian times, a lot of things changed, for example laws were passed that stopped children working in factories or as chimney sweeps. By the time Queen Victoria died, poor children such as Billy were much better cared for.

Young boys such as Billy were used as chimney sweeps because they were small enough to be sent up the chimneys.

LONDON — 'THE BIG SMOKE'

When Queen Victoria came to the throne in 1837, much of London was very unpleasant to live in. Big factories, using newly invented machines for making cloth and iron goods, were being built at a tremendous rate. Their huge chimneys belched out great clouds of black smoke and soot that hung in the air and settled around the workers' cramped houses, making it difficult to see or breathe.

Thousands of people flooded into London from the countryside looking for work, but there was no proper water supply or sewage system or organized rubbish collection. Many people, particularly in the centre of the city and in the east of London around Wapping and Bethnal Green, lived in appalling slums. The streets were crowded, busy and dirty. The dirt and sewage eventually found its way to the River Thames which, not

surprisingly, smelt terrible. Its banks were a very good home for rats.

For members of the upper classes, it was a different story. They lived further west, in Belgrave Square and Grosvenor Square for example, which are still fashionable areas today. Their houses were elegant, their roads were paved and they were surrounded by trees and parks — though their sewage system wasn't any better!

Gradually, people began to move out of the unhealthy centre of London, first to Camberwell and Clapham in the south, then to Highbury and Canonbury in the north. These were the first London suburbs.

By the end of Queen Victoria's reign in 1901, there were 4½ million people in London, which had grown to include many villages such as Westminster and Kensington that had formerly been outside London.

Despite its pollution, children known as mudlarks combed the banks of the Thames for bits and pieces they could sell for a few pence.

AT HOME

The children of rich parents certainly had a better time of it than poor children. They lived in large houses and had plenty to eat. But, even so, life was not as free and easy as it is to-day.

Father often ruled with great severity, and his wife, children and servants all had to obey him. Many upper-class families were very religious and said prayers together every day.

At other times children were kept out of sight in the nursery and looked after by a nanny until they were old enough to behave like adults in public. They spent more time with their nanny and other servants such as the cook, housemaid, butler and coachman, than with their parents.

Even large houses had no running water. If someone wanted to have a

The homes of the upper classes were very spacious.

bath, servants would have to fill the bath tub with jugs of hot water which was boiled in the kitchen.

Poor families often shared their houses with several others, and sometimes there were seven or eight people sleeping in one room. It was difficult to keep healthy.

Children were often neglected because their father would have to work twelve or more hours a day, and their mother would also try to get paid work to help bring in some money — perhaps matchbox making. Younger children would then be looked after by their older brothers and sisters, or sometimes just left to roam the streets. Few poor children

Poor homes usually consisted of a single room in which everything from cooking to sleeping was done.

went to school until after 1870.

The government didn't provide any houses, but some 'model dwellings' were built for the poor by ordinary people who wanted to help them. George Peabody, an American, gave money to build homes in London that were a great improvement on the slums. There was a tap and a lavatory on each floor which was shared among all the families. That was luxury! There are still Peabody buildings in London today, but each flat has a proper bathroom now.

GOING TO SCHOOL

Until the 1870 Education Act, no child had to go to school, and most poor children received no education at all. Children with well-to-do parents were taught at home by a private tutor or governess, and boys (they were considered more important in those days!) were often sent away to one of the public schools such as Eton, Harrow or Winchester. Conditions at these schools were very harsh and riots among the pupils were common.

Above *Victorian schoolmasters had a reputation for harshness. Some were kind. One tempted his pupils to come to school with hot potatoes.*

Below *The wealthy usually sent their children out of London to go to school at places like Rugby.*

These children at the Clare Market Ragged School, St Clement Danes, are being given their weekly free dinner.

Some businessmen wanted a different kind of education for their sons, so in the 1870s special commercial schools were founded. H.G. Wells, the author, went to Morley's Commercial Academy in Bromley, Kent, where the owner taught all the boys himself, concentrating on good handwriting, sums and book-keeping rather than Latin and classical studies.

Before 1870 poor children had to rely on 'ragged' or charity schools set up by churches. Many children had to work all week and then spend their one free day at Sunday school, where they read Bible stories. Teachers in the ragged schools often complained that the children were dirty and so hungry that they couldn't concentrate on their lessons.

After 1870 the government spent large sums of money on schools. The schools provided not only a basic education for all children, but also health checks and school clothes. So they were very important in improving conditions for the poor.

After 1891 free primary schooling was available and so was more widely used by poor families who could not afford school fees.

11

HEALTH AND DISEASE

An 1851 report showed that many working people died as young as twenty-five or thirty. Your own parents are probably older than that. Also, less than half the babies born in big cities reached the age of twenty. Thousands of babies and young children died. Some were accidentally given an overdose of a drug called opium used to make them sleep while their parents worked, and others died of malnutrition.

Children and their parents often died in factory accidents too. Gradually, laws were passed to improve working conditions and to clean up the streets, but even in the 1880s some people lived and worked in filth.

Doctors had to be paid for, because there was no National Health Service, so few poor people could afford to have treatment. Hospitals were simply places where people went to die.

It wasn't until the 1858 Medical Act that all doctors had to pass exams, so even rich people had to beware of 'quacks', who pretended to know how to cure them. And, without such things as antibiotics and immunization against measles or whooping cough, the children of the rich often died young too. That's one reason why Victorians often had six or seven children.

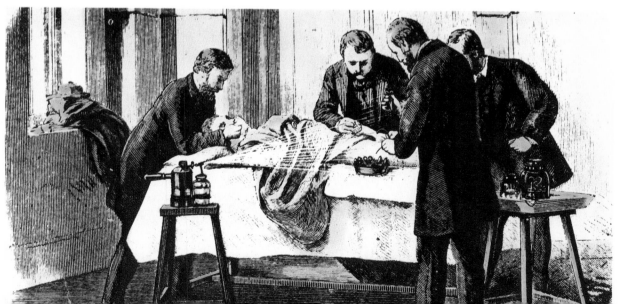

AT WORK

Above *This picture was used to show the wealthy what it was like to be a factory child.*

In the nineteenth century, goods made in British factories were in great demand. Britain was known as 'the workshop of the world'. But while factory owners became wealthy some kept their employees working in dreadful conditions.

In London children were often sent out to work as young as five years old and they might work from five or six in the morning until ten at night. If they fell asleep on the job they were beaten and if they were sick they weren't paid. Children only made one shilling (5p) a week, but every penny was vital to a poor family. No worker received sick pay until 1897. Paid holidays for some people only came in at the end of the century.

Children worked in match factories (dangerous, as the chemicals used caused jaw disease) printing and paper-staining factories. They also worked as tailors' apprentices, often in damp, dark basements. Even

Left *This family is making match boxes. They probably earned about 3p for a thousand boxes.*

children working at home suffered. They were kept up sewing until midnight or later, and had to be propped up or pinned to their mothers' skirts to stop them falling asleep.

Chimney sweeps like Billy had to climb up long, twisting, sooty chimneys to clean them with a long brush. Their elbows and knees would stream with blood, and their employers used to rub their wounds with salt and water to harden the skin.

Although a law was passed in 1840 to improve conditions, small boys were still used as chimney sweeps for many years after that. *The Water Babies* by Charles Kingsley is a heart-rending story about chimney sweeps.

Gradually, several Factory Acts were passed which limited the hours children could work and created factory inspectors to check up to see that employers obeyed the rules. But, even at the end of Queen Victoria's reign, working conditions were still much worse than they are today.

Tailors' apprentices worked in these sorts of conditions.

FOOD AND COOKING

Even as late as the 1890s, the diet of the poor in London consisted mainly of bread and dripping, jam, oatmeal, potatoes and tea. Some could afford meat, but in many houses there were no proper cooking facilities and water had to be brought from a pump at the end of the street and boiled on a fire. Many families took their Sunday joint to the baker's shop for cooking.

Poor children were last in the queue for food after the father and mother. The younger ones were sometimes sent out to scavenge in pig troughs for scraps. Few poor families ever saw fresh fruit, vegetables or milk, which were very expensive in towns, and so children often suffered from a lack of vitamins.

For the better-off workers and the upper classes, though, there were exciting developments in the later

nineteenth century. Margarine was invented in 1870 and cost only half the price of butter. Cheap food was by then being brought in from abroad. Housewives in towns could buy tinned, potted and preserved meat, fish and fruit.

A rich housewife rarely entered the kitchen. She left the ordering, cooking and serving of food to her servants, though she would keep an eye on how much money was spent. There were no refrigerators, freezers or food processors. Food was kept in an airy larder to keep cool.

Rich families had a large staff in the kitchen. Middle class families usually had at least a cook.

When the poor had meat to roast they often had to take it to the baker to be cooked.

CLOTHES

Victorian children had no play clothes. If they were well off, they were overdressed: girls were stuffed into thick stockings and tight long dresses and boys had to suffocate in velvet suits with restricting collars. You can imagine how difficult it was to run and jump bundled up like that. Jeans and T-shirts hadn't been thought of.

Women were not supposed to show their ankles, so their dresses brushed the ground. Fashionable women looked elegant walking through the park on Sundays holding a parasol in one hand and a smartly dressed little girl in the other. The trouble was that women working in factories wore long dresses too, and that was dangerous.

They would catch on the machines and cause nasty accidents. Women and girls all wore their hair long, usually tied back. They wore pinafores to protect their clothes, but never wore trousers.

Gentlemen wore top hats and swaggered along swinging their canes and bowing to the ladies. Working men wore flat hats and shirts and trousers.

Poor children had a few rags and nothing else. Sometimes they didn't even have shoes. Just think how cold their feet must have been in winter!

When bicycles became common in the 1870s, people, especially women, demanded looser and shorter clothes. Bathing suits covered most of the body and were a far cry from today's trunks and bikinis.

THE LAW

In Victorian London, many children were abandoned by their parents and lived in the streets. Some of these worked in gangs of pickpockets — stealing watches, silk handkerchiefs and purses from people in crowds. The Artful Dodger, in Charles Dickens's book, *Oliver Twist,* was a clever pickpocket. One Victorian writer described these children as 'very acute and ready witted, with a knowing twinkle in their eye'. But some children stole food because they were hungry.

Before 1850, when reform schools were founded, children caught committing crimes went to prison. One boy, Thomas Miller, had been to prison five times by the age of twelve, and had been whipped twice for thieving. As late as 1878 children of five and six were being sent to adult prisons.

Some children welcomed being sent to prison because they received clothes to wear, food to eat and a bed to sleep in. In 1852 one prison governor said that he thought some children had 'never been spoken to in a kind tone until they came into our gaol'.

Pickpockets, horse thiefs, forgers and muggers had to watch out for 'Peelers' — the first policemen, who were appointed by Sir Robert Peel in

1829. Policemen were very unpopular for many years. Drivers of horse-drawn cabs would lash out with their whips at policemen directing traffic, as they drove past.

Policemen rarely had time off and were punished with fines if they let a prisoner escape. They were expected to keep away from other working people. One policeman was fined 'for keeping company with singers on 24th and 25th December'.

'Peelers' were also known as 'bobbies', a name that has stuck.

BARNARDO'S HOMES

Many Victorian people did their best to help the poor and worked hard to get laws passed to improve conditions.

Thomas John Barnardo (1845-1905) was a very religious man who trained to be a doctor because he thought he wanted to do missionary work in China. Meanwhile, he opened a 'ragged school' for poor children in London.

One night a starving orphan, Jim Jarvis, knocked on Dr Barnardo's door and asked for help. He told him there were hundreds of children living on the streets of London and took him to see where they slept.

Lord Shaftsbury and Dr Barnardo finding homeless children sleeping in London's streets.

Dr Barnardo was appalled, and made speeches about these children to try and get the government to do something for them. Few politicians believed that such children existed. Then Lord Shaftesbury, a member of parliament who wanted to help the poor, went with Dr Barnardo late one night to Queen's Shields, Billingsgate. There, under a tarpaulin, they found seventy-three boys asleep.

A stranger sent Dr Barnardo £1000, asking him to open a home for poor boys. Dr Barnardo took this as a sign from God that he should abandon his plans to go to China. He stayed in London and opened his first home. Later he opened girls' homes too.

During his life Dr Barnardo helped over 60,000 children and his slogans were 'No destitute child ever refused admission' and 'The ever-open door'.

This portrait of Dr Barnardo was taken in about 1890.

HAVING FUN

There was no radio or television in Victorian homes, but people still managed to enjoy themselves. Families often played games together. Cards, blind man's buff, charades and team games were all popular and singsongs round the piano were a favourite pastime.

For an evening out, the well-to-do enjoyed dressing up to go to the theatre. Working people liked music halls where they could sing, watch comedy acts or see hypnotists at work.

Circuses were a popular form of entertainment in Victorian London.

Dancing bears, performing dogs and barrel organ players livened up the poorer streets. Parks offered amusements too. For a few pennies you could enjoy a peep show, or stare at a bearded lady or other 'freaks' in a little booth. *The Elephant Man* is a film which tells the story of a poor deformed person who was rescued by a doctor from such a sideshow.

Dogfights and cockfights, where animals fought to the death and people gambled on which would win, were very cruel. They were common for many years. Later they were replaced by sports such as football and cricket.

There were hundreds of gambling clubs in London. Rich and poor alike, all seem to have been addicted to betting money. They bet on horses, greyhounds, boxing matches, wrestling — almost anything!

Opposite   *A 'magic lantern' was an early type of slide projector that could flash pictures on to a screen. Seeing a magic lantern show was a great treat for Victorian children.*

THE GREAT EXHIBITION

On 1 May 1851, the gates of Hyde Park opened and thousands of people, who had camped in the streets overnight and cooked their breakfast on the pavement, streamed in to see The Great Exhibition which was housed in an enormous building called the Crystal Palace.

New British machinery, railway engineering and farming equipment, and hundreds of exotic, foreign works of art were all on show in this huge, fairy tale glass palace. Exhibitions and museums are common these days, but then it was a quite new idea.

It was Prince Albert, Queen Victoria's husband, who had decided to build a magnificent showpiece to make British people proud of their

The British colonies were represented at The Great Exhibition.

work and impress the world. Two thousand workmen had been employed to build the palace, which was 272 m (892 ft) long and used 92,900 sq m (999,976 sq ft) of glass!

Schoolchildren, businessmen and farming families from the country, all enjoyed a day out at the Crystal Palace, and the exhibition attracted foreign tourists too. Altogether, six million people visited The Great Exhibition before it closed in the autumn of 1851.

Then the Crystal Palace was moved to Sydenham in South London. It was badly damaged by fire in 1854 and finally burnt down in another fire in 1936.

The nineteenth century had been troubled with wars abroad and much unrest and rioting in Britain because

The Crystal Palace was a great technical achievement.

The opening of The Great Exhibition at the Crystal Palace.

of bad working conditions and poverty. Queen Victoria called the Great Exhibition 'The greatest triumph of peace which the world has ever seen'.

Unfortunately, more wars lay ahead, but even so the Exhibition was a great achievement. With the money it made — £186,000 — Prince Albert arranged for permanent museums, including the Victoria and Albert and the Natural History Museums, to be built in Kensington.

A Day at the Seaside

Before the building of the railways, it was only the rich who could afford to travel from London to the seaside for a holiday. But from the 1840s onwards, more and more working people enjoyed a trip to Margate or Brighton. By the 1870s it was possible to take a family of four on a day excursion to Brighton for as little as nine shillings (45p). Most people could manage to save this sum up. During the 1860s, as many as 30,000 visitors would arrive on Brighton beach on a Bank Holiday.

For family entertainment, Brighton was hard to beat. You could bathe in the sea, stroll along the piers, hear a band play, buy souvenirs at the kiosks or have your photograph taken. There were concerts to listen to, puppet shows to laugh at and plays to see.

In the 1880s and 1890s there were even more exciting things to do. Magnus Volk built a little electric railway along Brighton seafront and a 'motor rail' out to Devil's Dyke on the South Downs. You could then take the funicular to the top and have a thrilling trip back in a cable car.

A day at the seaside was very important at a time when few people had any paid holidays. Some trippers became very excited and rowdy and Brighton got a reputation for being a rough and noisy town!

Left *Ramsgate was another popular Victorian seaside resort.*

Right *Railway stations, such as Brighton built of glass, cast iron and brick, were one of the great architectural achievements of the nineteenth century.*

THE END OF AN ERA

Queen Victoria died in 1901. She had come to the throne in 1837 and during her long reign Britain had undergone many changes. Conditions for children had improved dramatically. By the end of her reign, children were better housed, better clothed and better educated than ever before. This was partly due to improved living conditions, increased prosperity and technical developments, but it was also because attitudes towards children had begun to change. This could be seen in the laws that were passed in the second half of the nineteenth century, for example the 1870 Education Act and the various factory acts.

Upper-class children also benefitted from this change in attitude. They now enjoyed a closer, warmer relationship with their parents and public schools treated their pupils better.

By the time Queen Victoria died most children could look forward to a much more comfortable and more pleasant life than was possible at the beginning of her reign.

The funeral of Queen Victoria represented the end of an era.

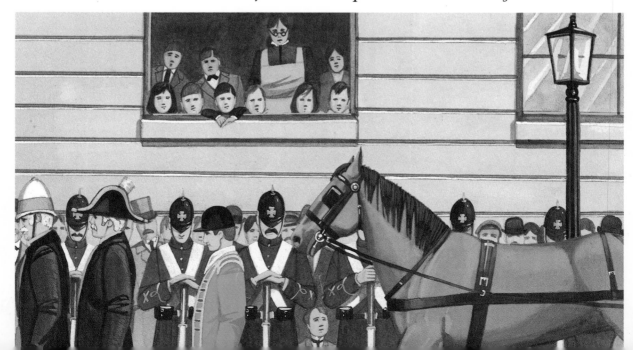

GLOSSARY

Anaesthetic   A kind of medicine used to put people to sleep before an operation.

Antibiotics   Medicines, such as penicillin, drunk or injected to kill germs.

Antiseptics   Creams or liquids containing a substance that kills germs in a cut or wound.

Commercial schools   Schools which teach subjects useful for business, such as typewriting and book-keeping.

Diet   What people usually eat.

Dripping   Fat collected from a piece of meat while it cooks, usually spread on bread and eaten.

Funicular railway   Train on a special track that climbs a steep hill.

Government   The people running the country.

Immunization   An injection that stops you getting certain diseases.

Nanny   A servant who looks after young children.

Pinafore   A long apron.

'Quack'   A person who pretends to be a doctor.

Ragged schools   Schools for poor children set up by churches.

Sewage   Dirty water and waste from kitchens and lavatories.

Sewage system   A network of pipes for removing dirty water and waste from kitchens and lavatories.

Squalid   Dirty and unpleasant.

Welfare state   Where the government provides housing, health care, schooling and many other things for people.

MORE BOOKS TO READ

Penelope Davies, *Children of the Industrial Revolution* (Wayland, 1972)

Molly Harrison, *Growing up in Victorian Days* (Wayland, 1980)

Sir Charles Petrie, *Great Beginnings in the Age of Queen Victoria* (Macmillan, 1967)

Stewart Ross, *A Victorian Factory Worker* (Wayland, 1985)

Sallie Purkis, *At Home and in the Streets in 1900* (Longman, 1981)

Sallie Purkis and Elizabeth Merson, *At School and in the Country in 1900* (Longman, 1981)

W.J. Reader, *Life in Victorian England* (Batsford, 1964)

INDEX

Albert, Prince 26-7
Anaesthetics 13, 31
Antiseptics 13

Barnardo, Dr Thomas John
    22-3
Bathing suits 19
Bicycles 19
'Bobbies' 21
Brighton 28-9

Chimney sweeps 4, 5, 15
Cricket 24
Crystal Palace 26-7

Diet 4, 16, 17, 31
Disraeli, Benjamin 4

Education Acts 10, 30
Elephant Man, The 24

Factories 6
    accidents 13, 18-19
    conditions 14-15
Football 24

Funicular 28, 31

Gambling 24
Games 24

Jarvis, Jim 22

Magic lantern show 24-5
Margarine 17
Match making 14
'Model dwellings' 9
Museums 27

Nanny 31

Oliver Twist 20

Peabody George 9
Peel, Sir Robert 20
'Peelers' 20-21
Police 20-21
Pollution 6-7

Quacks 13, 31

Railways 28-29
Religion 8

Servants 8, 31
Sewage system 6, 31
Schools 10
    'ragged' 11, 31
    commercial 11, 31
Shaftsbury, Lord 23
Suburbs 7

Thames 6

Victoria, Queen 4, 5, 6, 30
    funeral 30

Wages 14
Water Babies, The 15

Picture Acknowledgements

The pictures in this book were supplied by the following: Barnardo Photographic Archive 23; BBC Hulton Picture Archive 10 (bottom); Commissioner of the Police of the Metropolis 21; E.T. Archive 24, 26; The Mansell Collection 27 (right); Mary Evans Picture Library 27 (left), 28; Ann Ronan Picture Library 11; The remaining pictures are from the Wayland Picture Library.